Real Science-4-Kids

Teacher's Manual

Pre-Level I

Dr. R. W. Keller

RealScience 4 Kids

Cover design: David Keller
Opening page: David Keller, Rebecca Keller
Illustrations: Rebecca Keller

Copyright © 2004, 2007 Gravitas Publications, Inc.

Real Science-4-Kids: Chemistry Pre-Level I Teacher's Manual

ISBN 0-9765097-2-5

Published by Gravitas Publications, Inc.
P.O. Box 4790
Albuquerque, NM 87196-4790

Printed in United States

A note from the author

This curriculum is designed to provide an introduction to Chemistry for students in kindergarten through third grade. The student laboratory manual is intended to be the first step in developing a framework for real science. The series of experiments in the laboratory manual will help the students develop the skills for the first step in the scientific method: making good observations.

There are four sections in each chapter. Section I: "Think about it" provides questions for the students to think about before they begin the experiment. Section II: "Test it" directs the students in setting up the experiment, collecting any data, and observing what happens. Section III: "What did you discover?" gives the students an opportunity to summarize the observations they have made. Section IV: "Why" provides a short explanation for what they may or may not have observed.

The experiments take up to 1 hour. The materials needed for each experiment are given on the next page.

Enjoy!

R. W. Keller

Materials at a Glance

All of the materials needed for each experiment are given in the following chart:

Experiment 1	Experiment 2	Experiment 3	Experiment 4	Experiment 5	Experiment 6	Experiment 7	Experiment 8	Experiment 9	Experiment 10
magnifying glass cotton balls rubber bands pencil crackers cheese marshmallow bean color-coated candy (such as M&Ms)	Legos small marshmallows large marshmallows toothpicks	plastic cups measuring cup lemon juice vinegar milk baking soda water	plastic cups measuring cup white grape juice grapefruit juice lemon juice milk baking soda mineral water antacid tablet one head red cabbage distilled water	plastic cups measuring cup lemon juice vinegar baking soda mineral water antacid tablet one head red cabbage distilled water	plastic cups milk water juice oil melted butter liquid soap	plastic cups small rocks Legos sand sugar salt water food coloring coffee filters pencil tape	ripe banana green banana pretzels or salty crackers raw potatoes cooked potatoes blindfold	plastic cups Elmer's white glue liquid laundry starch paper clips	active dry yeast sugar vegetable oil flour measuring cups measuring spoons marking pen two bowls

Contents

Experiment 1

What is it made of?

Materials needed:

magnifying glass
household items such as
- cotton balls
- rubber bands
- pencil

several food items such as
- crackers
- cheese
- marshmallow
- bean
- color-coated candy (such as M&Ms)

In this unit, the students will be introduced to *atoms*. Atoms are the building blocks of all things.

The objectives of this lesson are (1) to help younger students make careful observations by noticing details and (2) to develop a vocabulary to describe their observations.

I. Think about it.
II. Test it.

In this experiment the students think about an object, such as a cracker, a piece of cheese, or a candy, and then observe the object. **Without allowing the students to look at the object,** help them describe the object, using both words and pictures.   Direct their inquiry with questions. For example

What color is a cracker?
Is a cracker hard (like a plastic toy) or soft (like a feather)?
Is a cracker large (like an elephant) or small (like a mouse)?
Is a cracker smooth (like a marble) or rough (like sandpaper)?

Their answers may look something like this:

cracker

Describe and draw what you think.	Describe and draw what you see.
brown *round* *scratchy* *crumbly*	

Next, have the students look carefully at the object. Using the magnifying glass, have them examine the object and make careful observations. Ask them if the object looks different than they thought. Direct their investigation with questions such as the following:

Is the cracker as large (or as small) as you thought?
Is the cracker smooth or rough?
What color is the cracker? Is it exactly brown? or white? Does it have other colors in it?
What happens to the cracker if you break it in half? Is it the same on the inside as on the outside?
What does the cracker look like under the magnifying glass? Can you describe what you see?

Often students discover that they have not seen or thought about some detail in an object. For example, sometimes crackers have holes on the top. This may be an observation they have never noticed. Or there may be stripes or speckles in the cracker they haven't noticed. Also, they can observe that some things are the same on the inside, like crackers and cotton balls, but other things are not the same on the inside, like color-coated candy or pinto beans.

cracker

Describe and draw what you think.	Describe and draw what you see.
brown round scratchy crumbly	white and brown speckles
	holes on top

Have them repeat this exercise with two or three more objects. Remember to have the students describe the item first without looking at it. They can do as many items as they want, describing the item first without looking at it and then carefully observing the item using a magnifying glass.

III. What did you discover?

The questions can be answered verbally or in writing, depending on the writing ability of the student. With these questions help the students think about their observations. Help them see where an observation was the *same* as what they thought and where an observation was *different*.

IV. Why?

Read Section IV with the students and discuss why their observations may have been different from what they thought.

Experiment 2

Follow the rules!

Materials needed:

   Legos
   small and large marshmallows
   toothpicks

In this experiment, the students will explore how the building blocks of matter (atoms) fit together to make molecules.

The objective of this lesson is to help students understand that matter is made of smaller units (called atoms) and atoms follow specific rules when forming molecules.

Place the Legos on the table and have the students look at them. Show the students how each Lego has a certain number of holes on one side and the same number of pegs on the other side.

Direct the student's inquiry with questions such as the following:

1. How many Legos can you put together with the 2-pegged Lego?

2. How many Legos can you put together with the 4-pegged Lego?

3. How many Legos can you put together with the 16-pegged Lego?

Help the students understand that because Legos have only a certain number of pegs and a certain number of holes, only a certain number of structures can be built.

Compare the Legos to atoms. Help the students understand that atoms are like Legos in that they can only hook to other atoms in certain ways.

I. What do you think?

Help the students answer the questions in Section I of their workbook.

II. Test it.

Now have the students make "molecules" with the marshmallows. First they will make as many molecules as they can without any rules. Have them make several and then draw one. Next, have them apply a "rule" to the big marshmallow. The rule is: the big marshmallow can only use three sticks. Their answers may look something like this:

Make as many "molecules" as you can with the marshmallows.	Now, the big marshmallow can only use three sticks. Make as many molecules as you can following this rule.
How many can you make? _10_	How many can you make? __5__
Can you draw one?	Can you draw one? 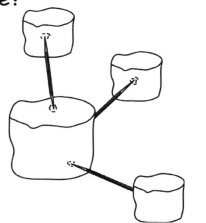

Next, have the students make "molecules" using the following rules : two sticks and one stick for the big marshmallow. Have them write down the number of molecules they can make. Have them draw one.

Their answers may look something like this:

Now, the big marshmallow can only use two sticks. Make as many molecules as you can following this rule.

How many can you make? ____3____

Can you draw one?

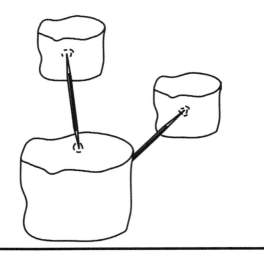

Now, the big marshmallow can only use one stick. Make as many molecules as you can following this rule.

How many can you make? ____1____

Can you draw one?

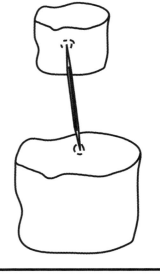

Have the students compare the molecules they made without the rules to the molecules they made with the rules. Help the students answer the questions in Section III. Help them see that by following the rules they were able to make fewer molecules than when they didn't follow the rules. Explain to them that it is important for atoms to follow rules. Discuss Section IV with the students. Help them understand that when we don't follow rules, there is no order. There is chaos. Help them see that the same thing would be true if atoms did not follow rules.

Experiment 3

What will happen?

Materials needed:

plastic cups
measuring cup
the following food items:

- lemon juice
- vinegar
- milk
- baking soda
- water

In this unit, the students will observe chemical reactions.

Experiment Set-up:

1. Label the plastic cups (A), (B), (C), and (D).

2. Pour 1/4 cup of lemon juice into cup (A).

3. Pour 1/4 cup of vinegar into cup (B).

4. Pour 1/4 cup of milk into cup (C).

5. Pour 1/4 cup of water into cup (D) and add two tablespoons of baking soda. Mix until it is completely dissolved.

Experiment:

Set the cups out on the table for the students. Do not let them know what is in each.

Have them examine the contents inside the cups. They should observe the color, smell, and taste. Have them write what they have observed, or record the answers for them.

1. Cups (A) and (B)

Ask the students what they think will happen if they add cup (A) to cup (B). Write down their guess.

Next have them pour cup (B) into cup (A). Have them observe and record what happens.

Vinegar and lemon juice do not react, so they should not observe much happening.

Rinse the cups with water.

Refill cup (B) with 1/4 cup of vinegar. Refill cup (A) with 1/4 cup of lemon juice.

2. Cups (A) and (C)

Next, ask the students what they think will happen if they add cup (A) to cup (C). Write down their answers.

Have them pour the contents of cup (A) into cup (C). Help them record what happens. The lemon juice will curdle the milk. The students will observe clumps forming in the milk as the milk curdles. This is a chemical reaction. The clumps are protein in the milk that have been denatured by the lemon juice. The clumps form a *precipitate* [pre•cip'•i•tate].

Rinse the cups with water.

Refill cup (A) with 1/4 of lemon juice. Refill cup (C) and with 1/4 cup of milk.

3. Cups (A) and (D)

Next ask the students what they think will happen if they add cup (A) to cup (D). Write down their answers.

Have them pour the contents of cup (A) into cup (D). Help them record what happens. They should observe a chemical reaction occuring between the lemon juice and the baking soda. The chemical reaction gives off bubbles which should be visible. If this does not happen, pour out the contents of cup (D). Make a new mixture of water and baking soda and add twice as much baking soda. It doesn't matter whether or not all of the baking soda is dissolved.

Rinse the cups with water.

Refill cup (D) with 1/4 cup baking soda water.

4. Cups (B) and (C)

Next, ask the students what they think will happen if they add cup (B) to cup (C). Write down their answers.

Have them pour the contents of cup (B) into cup (C). Help them record what happens. They should observe a chemical reaction similar to step 2. The vinegar should cause the milk to curdle.

Rinse the cups with water.

Refill cup (B) with 1/4 of vinegar. Refill cup (C) and with 1/4 cup of milk.

5. Cups (B) and (D)

Next, ask the students what they think will happen if they add cup (B) to cup (D). Write down their answers.

Have them pour the contents of cup (B) into cup (D). Help them record what happens. They should observe a chemical reaction similar to step 3. The vinegar and baking soda should react and the mixture should give off bubbles.

Rinse the cups with water.

Refill cup (B) with 1/4 of vinegar. Refill cup (D) with 1/4 cup of baking soda water.

6. Cups (C) and (D)

Next, ask the students what they think will happen if they add cup (C) to cup (D). Write down their answers.

Have them pour the contents of cup (C) into cup (D). Help them record what happens. They should not observe any chemical reaction taking place. The milk will not curdle, nor will there be any visible bubbles nor other signs of a chemical reaction taking place.

Have the students pour out the contents of cup (D) and clean up the experiment space.

Summary – Have the students summarize their results. The answers are provided below.

1. Did lemon juice (A) react with vinegar (B)?_____no_____

2. Did lemon juice (A) react with milk (C)? ____yes_____

3. Did lemon juice (A) react with baking soda (D)? _____yes_____

4. Did vinegar (B) react with milk (C)? ____yes_____

5. Did vinegar (B) react with baking soda (D)? ____yes_____

6. Did milk (C) react with baking soda (D)? _____no_____

III. Help the students answer the questions in Section III. Their answers may vary.

IV. Discuss the similarities and differences among the four liquids. Explain to the students that vinegar and lemon juice are similar kinds of molecules and that milk and baking soda are not similar. Explain that although lemon juice and vinegar are not identical, they behave in similar ways because they are similar kinds of molecules.

Experiment 4

Sour or not sour?

Materials needed:

plastic cups
measuring cup
the following food items:

- white grape juice
- lemon juice
- grapefruit juice
- milk
- baking soda
- mineral water
- alka-seltzer tablets
- one head of red cabbage
- distilled water

To do 1 hour before:

Chop or shred the head of red cabbage and boil in 4-6 cups of distilled water for 15 minutes. Remove cabbage and allow liquid to cool to room temperature.

[NOTE: Do not use tap water. Use only *distilled water* or you will not get the correct results]

In this experiment, the students will explore the properties of acids and bases. They will taste several food items to determine which foods are sour tasting and which are not. They will then use an acid-base indicator, red cabbage juice, to show how acids turn pink and bases turn green with the indicator.

This experiment requires that the students sample both acids and bases. It is relatively easy to find foods that are acidic, but much more difficult to find foods that are basic. The only two safe products that we could find which are basic are baking soda water and antacids. Most household cleaning products are basic, but these are not listed since they are not safe to taste.

I. Think about it.

First have the students make predictions about which liquids will be sour to taste and which will not be sour. Have them mark their predictions where indicated on the table given. Their answers will vary.

II. Test it.

Pour 1/4 cup of each liquid into plastic cups. For the baking soda water add 1 teaspoon baking soda to 1/4 cup of water in a plastic cup. For the antacid, add one tablet to 1/4 cup of water in a plastic cup.

Next have the students taste the liquids and mark which are sour and which are not sour. Help them try to distinquish between "sour" and "bitter." The mineral water, baking soda water will taste "bad," but not sour. They are bitter or salty. The antacid water will taste sweet. Also, white grape juice will be sweet and not necessarily sour. Let them decide if they think it is sour or not.

Their answers may look as follows:

Liquid	sour	not sour
white grape juice		X
milk		X
lemon juice	X	
grapefruit juice	X	
mineral water		X
antacid		X
water		X
baking soda water		X

Tear out the pages labeled "SOUR" and "NOT SOUR" and place them on the table.
After the students taste the liquids, have them place the cups on the appropriate labeled pages.

Next, pour the red cabbage juice that you made earlier into a measuring cup. Have the students add 1/4 cup of red cabbage juice to each liquid they tasted. Have them observe the colors of each liquid. They will be asked if the color changes. They are looking for the color change *of the cabbage juice*. The natural color of the cabbage juice is a deep red-purple. It will change to pink, green, or light purple in the liquids. Have the students record their results.

Expected results should look like the following:

Liquid	Color change? (yes or no)	What is the color?
white grape juice	yes	pink
milk	no	purple
lemon juice	yes	pink
grapefruit juice	yes	pink
mineral water	yes/no	light purple
antacid	yes	green
water	no	purple
baking soda water	yes	green

Help the students answer the questions in Section III. Their answers will vary. Example answers are given.

III. What did you discover?

Which liquids were sour? *the lemon juice and grapefruit juice*

Which liquids were not sour? *the milk, water, and mineral water*

What color did the "sour" liquids turn when you added the cabbage juice?

pink

What color did the "not-so-sour" liquids turn when you added the cabbage juice?

green or purple

Why do you think the "sour" liquid and "not-so-sour" liquids turned the cabbage juice different colors?
They have different types of molecules.

If you added cabbage juice to a drink and it turned pink, do you think that drink would taste sour?
yes

Discuss Section IV with the students. Have them think about why some of the liquids turned the cabbage juice pink and some liquids turned the cabbage juice green. Explain to them that the liquids that turned the cabbage juice pink are called *acids* and the liquids that turned the cabbage juice green are called *bases*.

Explain to the students that cabbage juice is an *indicator*. Tell them that an indicator is anything that tells you something. For example, a gas gauge in the car could be called an indicator - it tells you the level of gas in the tank. The thermostat in the house could be called an indicator - it tells you the temperature of the room.

The term indicator in chemistry refers to a chemical that tells you something about other chemicals. Cabbage juice is an *acid-base indicator*.

Explain to the students that cabbage juice will always turn pink in acids and will always turn green in bases, unless there is something wrong with the indicator. Some liquids, like milk and water do not turn the indicator another color. Explain that these liquids are called *neutral* and that they are neither acids nor bases.

Experiment 5

Pink and green together

Materials needed:

plastic cups
measuring cup
the following food items:

- lemon juice
- vinegar
- baking soda
- mineral water
- antacid tablets
- one head of red cabbage
- distilled water

To do 1 hour before:

Chop or shred the head of red cabbage and boil in 4-6 cups of distilled water for 15 minutes. Remove cabbage and allow liquid to cool to room temperature.

[NOTE: Do not use tap water. Use only *distilled water* or you will not get the correct results]

In the last experiment the students added red cabbage juice to several liquids to determine which were acids and which were bases. In this experiment the students will explore what happens when an acid is added to a base and when a base is added to an acid.

Set up four plastic cups with 1/4 cup of the following:

(1) vinegar

(2) lemon juice

(3) mineral water

(4) distilled water

Take two more plastic cups and add 1/4 cup of water. Add 1 teaspoon of baking soda to one and an antacid tablet to the other.

I. Think about it.

Have the students think about and answer the questions in Section I. Their answers will vary.

II. Test it.

Place all of the cups on the table and have the students add 1/4 cup cabbage juice to each cup. Have them observe the colors of each cup. Help them record their results in the chart. They should get the following:

Liquid	Pink	Green	Purple
distilled water			X
mineral water			X
lemon juice	X		
vinegar	X		
baking soda water		X	
antacid water		X	

Next, have the students add the liquids together. Help them record any color changes. For example when lemon juice [pink] is added to mineral water [purple] the mineral water will turn pink. When mineral water [purple] is added to baking soda water [green] the color may change only slightly. Encourage the students to keep pouring the liquids back and forth.

Their answers may look like this:

	antacid water	lemon juice	vinegar	mineral water	distilled water	baking soda water
antacid water		*antacid to lemon juice --> pink to green*				
lemon juice	*lemon juice to antacid --> green to pink*					
vinegar				*vinegar to mineral water --> purple to pink*		
mineral water			*mineral water to vinegar --> stays pink*			
distilled water						
baking soda water						

III. What did you discover?

Help the students answer the questions in Section III. They should have seen some of the pink liquids turn green when green was added and some of the green liquids turn pink when pink was added.

The last question asks what color all of the liquids turned when they were finished. In the end all of the liquids should have turned purple. If some liquids are still green or pink, have the students pour them back and forth until every cup is purple.

IV. Why?

Discuss the results with the students. Explain to them that when they added the liquids back and forth, the colors changed because the acids and bases were *reacting* with each other. Remind the students that Chapter 3 tells us a reaction is "indicated" by a color change. In this case the cabbage juice indicator changes color as the acids react with the bases and when the bases are added to the acids.

At the end of the experiment all of the liquids turn purple. Explain to the students that the acids and bases react with each other and cancel each other out. In the end there are no acids or bases left, only neutral liquids.

Experiment 6

Make it mix!

```
Materials needed:

    plastic cups
    the following food items:

            • milk
            • water
            • juice
            • oil
            • melted butter
            • liquid soap
```

In this experiement the students will observe mixtures. They will see how liquids that are similar will mix and liquids that are not similar will not mix.

I. Think about it.

Help the students answer the questions in Section I. Have them think about what might happen if they added milk to water, milk to juice, or water to oil. Their answers may vary. Help them record their answers in the blanks provided.

II. Test it.

Help the students set up Section II. In two sets of plastic cups, have the students add 1/2 cup of the following:

water in 2 of the cups

milk in 2 of the cups

juice in 2 of the cups

oil in 2 of the cups

melted butter in 2 of the cups

Using a third cup as the test cup, have the students pour a little (1/8 cup) water into a little (1/8 cup) milk. Have them observe what happens and then record their results. Help them identify when two liquids mix. When two liquids mix, they won't be able to tell where one liquid starts and the other ends. When they don't mix, droplets of one liquid will be visible in the other.

Make sure they do not confuse a color change with "not mixing." The liquids could change colors, but should be considered "mixed" if there are no droplets visible.

It is not necessary to test every combination. At a minimum have the students test oil and water, oil and milk, and oil and butter.

Their results should be as follows:

	water	milk	juice	oil	butter
water	mixed	mixed	mixed	not mixed --> oil droplets visible	not mixed --> butter droplets visible
milk	mixed	mixed	mixed	slightly mixed	slightly mixed
juice	mixed	mixed	mixed	not mixed --> oil droplets visible	not mixed --> butter droplets visible
oil	not mixed --> oil droplets visible	slightly mixed	not mixed --> oil droplets visible	mixed	mixed
butter	not mixed --> butter droplets visible	slightly mixed	not mixed --> butter droplets visible	mixed	mixed

II. Test it. (continued) — Test it with soap.

Have the students repeat the experiment with soap. Using the same cups, add 1 teaspoon of liquid soap to one set of cups. The students should observe that soap doesn't change the liquids that already mix [e.g. water and juice], but makes the oil "mix" a little better into water and juice. Their results will vary, but may look as follows:

	water	milk	juice	oil	butter
water + soap	*mixed*	*mixed*	*mixed*	*somewhat mixed*	*somewhat mixed*
milk + soap	*mixed*	*mixed*	*mixed*	*somewhat mixed*	*somewhat mixed*
juice + soap	*mixed*	*mixed*	*mixed*	*somewhat mixed*	*somewhat mixed*
oil + soap	*somewhat mixed*	*somewhat mixed*	*somewhat mixed*	*mixed*	*mixed*
butter + soap	*somewhat mixed*	*somewhat mixed*	*somewhat mixed*	*mixed*	*mixed*

III. What did you discover?

Help the students answer the questions in Section III. They should have observed that oil and butter do not mix with either water or juice. They also should have observed that oil mixes somewhat with milk and better with butter.

By adding soap, the students should have observed that oil mixes a little better with water and juice and much better with milk and butter.

IV. Why?

Discuss Section IV with the students. Explain to them that "similar" liquids mix well and liquids that are not "similar" do not mix well. Juice is similar to water because juice is mostly water, so juice and water mix well. Milk is a colloid, but will still mix well with water and juice, because milk is mostly water. [A colloid is a mixture that has very small droplets of molecules that do not actually mix well, but the droplets are so small it looks mixed. Colloids are often opaque]. Oil and butter are similar because both oil and butter are fats. Oil and water are not similar, so oil will not mix well with either water or juice.

Explain the "rule," that similar liquids mix and dissimilar liquids do not mix.

Explain that soap is both a little bit like water and a little bit like oil, so soap mixes in both types of liquids. Because soap is like both water and oil it "dissolves" oil in water. This is why soap works as a cleaner.

Experiment 7

Make it un-mix!

Materials needed:

    plastic cups
    several small rocks (5-10)
    Legos
    bag of sand
    sugar
    salt
    water
    food coloring
    coffee filters
    pencil
    tape

In this experiment the students will see how to separate various mixtures. They will first explore ways to separate mixtures such as legos and pebbles. They will then explore ways to separate more complicated mixtures such as salt and sugar. Finally they will learn a new technique, called *paper chromatography,* for separating different colors.

I. Think about it.

Discuss the questions in Section I with the students. Help them think of ways they might separate several different mixtures. Their answers may vary. Encourage them to think of different "tools," such as a sieve or flour sifter for separating mixtures. Also encourage them to think of using water to dissolve part of a mixture, such as salt in the salt-sand mixture.

II. Test it.

Now have the students test one or more of their own ideas. Even if you know their idea won't work, let them test it. Possible answers as follows:

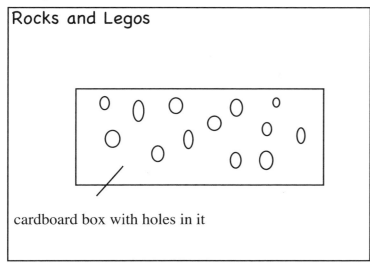

Rocks and Legos

cardboard box with holes in it

Use hands and fingers to un-mix the rocks from the Legos.

Use a cardboard box with holes in it to un-mix the rocks from the Legos

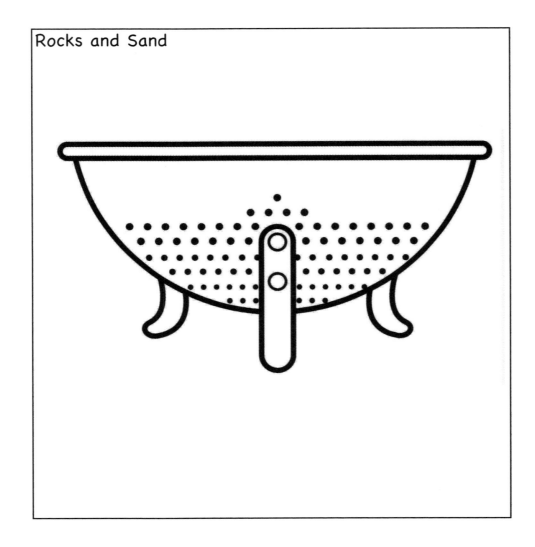

Rocks and Sand

Use a sieve to separate rocks and sand.

Use a hair dryer to blow away all of the sand.

Sand and Salt

salt water

sand

Use a cheesecloth to separate rocks and sand.

Use water to dissolve the salt.

Salt and Sugar

Use ants at a picnic.
[This is just for fun.]
Since ants like sugar better
than salt, the ants will carry off
the sugar and leave the salt.

The next sample involves separating different colors of food coloring. Have the students place several drops of different food coloring into 1/2 cup of water. The resulting color should be black or deep brown. Discuss with the students possible ways to separate the colors.

Next discuss a new method of separating colored water — "chromatography" [chro'•ma•tog'•ra•phy]. Explain to the students that they can separate the colors using a piece of coffee filter paper.

Help the students set up the chromatography sample. Have them cut the filter paper into long strips. Have them tape one end of one strip to the pencil and place the pencil over the glass with the colored water, letting the paper strip dip into the water. They should immediately observe the water begin to migrate up the paper strip. They should detect the green food coloring migrate first, followed by the blue, then yellow, and finally red.

When they take the paper strip out of the water, have them lay it down on another piece of white paper. They should easily see the different colors.

Have them repeat the experiment with an "unknown." Without the students observing, add several drops of two or three colors into a glass with water. Give the glass to the students and let them perform paper chromatography to determine which colors are in the cup. Have the students prepare an "unknown" for the teacher, and let the teacher determine the colors in the cup. This is very fun and can be repeated as many times as wanted.

III. What did you discover?

Help the students answer the questions in Section III. Their answers will vary.

IV. Why?

Discuss Section IV with the students. Explain to them that there are many different ways to separate mixtures. Review the different ways they discovered to separate their mixtures.

Discuss with the students why some mixtures are easier to separate than other mixtures. Mixtures that have small components and mixtures that are made of similar items are harder to separate than mixtures with larger components and dissimilar items. Explain that scientists use a variety of tools and techniques to separate mixtures. The "trick" called chromatography is a technique frequently used by scientists to separate a variety of molecules. Explain to the students that this technique can be used to separate different kinds of molecules, such as proteins or DNA, and not just molecules that make color.

Experiment 8

Salty or sweet!

Materials needed:	To Do 1 Hour Before:

the following food items:
  • ripe banana
  • green banana
  • pretzels or salty crackers
  • raw potatoes
  • cooked potatoes
  • other food items
blindfold
	Boil one or two raw potatoes for 15-20 minutes and mash them.

In this experiment the students will explore how foods flavored by different molecules taste different. Without tasting, they will be asked to separate foods that are salty from foods that are sweet or foods that are neither salty nor sweet. They will then put on a blindfold and by tasting the foods again, determine which foods are salty, which are sweet, and which are neither. They will see that it is easy to determine salty, sweet, or even sour foods but not as easy to identify foods which are "NEITHER."

I. Think about it.

Ask the students to think about the questions in Section I. Help them record their answers. Their answers may vary.

II. Test it.

Have the students tear out the pages labeled "SALTY," "SWEET," and "NEITHER" and spread them out on the table.

Next, have the students guess, without tasting, which foods will be salty, which will be sweet, and which will be neither. Have them place the foods on the corresponding pages.

Now take a blindfold and cover the students' eyes. Hand them one of the items from one of the pages, and ask them to guess if it is a sweet item, a salty item, or neither. If they guess correctly place the item back on the labeled paper. If their guess was incorrect, place the item off to the side.

When they finish tasting the items, remove the blindfold and have them see how many items they guessed correctly.

III. What did you discover?

Discuss the questions in Section III with the students. Help them record their answers. Ask them how many foods they guessed correctly and how many they didn't guess correctly. Their answers may vary.

IV. Why?

Explain to the students that the flavors we taste in foods come from different molecules. Also explain to them that their tongue is designed to detect the different flavors in foods. Explain that the taste buds on the tongue can tell the salt molecules from the sugar molecules.

Discuss with the students how foods such as potatoes and green bananas contain long chains of sugar molecules called carbohydrates [car'bo•hy'drate']. Because the sugar molecules in carbohydrates are hooked together in long chains taste buds cannot detect them.   This is why raw potatoes and green bananas do not taste very sweet. Explain to the students that when potatoes or bananas are cooked, the cooked food is sweeter than the uncooked food. Explain that cooking breaks apart carbohydrates [the long chain of sugar molecules], and so their taste buds can detect the sugar.

Experiment 9

Making goo!

Materials needed:

> Elmer's white glue
> liquid laundry starch
> plastic cups
> paper clips (30)

In this experiment the students will explore the chemical reaction between Elmer's glue and liquid laundry starch. The students will observe how the properties of the Elmer's glue changes when liquid laundry starch is added.

I. Think about it.

Help the students think about the questions in Section I. They can give their answers orally, or they can record their answers in the space provided. Their answers may vary.

II. Test it.

Help the students set up the experiment. They will be adding liquid laundry starch to Elmer's glue. Help the students add glue to the paper cup. It is important not to put too much glue in the cup since an excess of laundry starch is needed. Help the students add the laundry starch. Nothing will happen without the students kneading the glue and starch mixture. Encourage the students to knead the mixture with their fingers. This is messy for teachers, but delightful for most students. Both the glue and laundry starch are nontoxic and can easily be cleaned from clothing and hands.

As the students knead the mixture, help them think about what changes they may be observing. They should feel the glue become less sticky and more rubbery. They should be able to get the glue to roll into a ball or flatten in their hands like a pancake.

III. What did you discover?

Help the students answer the questions in Section III. They should have noticed a significant change in the properties of the glue when the starch was added. Help them describe what they observed.

IV. Why?

The glue and the laundry starch are both *polymers*. Polymers are long chains of molecules hooked together. When these two polymers are added together, a chemical reaction changes the properties of the polymers. In this case, the laundry starch makes the long chains in the glue hook to each other. This is called *crosslinking* because it makes cross-links.

To illustrate this principle, gather 30 paper clips. Have the students make three chains with 10 paper clips each. Have the students lay them side by side on the table. Show the students that they can slide the paper clips past each other. Explain that this is how the glue behaves without the laundry starch. Now take the paper clips and hook two or three from one chain to two or three from another chain. This is a cross-link. Next show the students that they cannot easily slide the chains back and forth with respect to each other. This illustrates the changes that occur when the laundry starch is added to the glue.

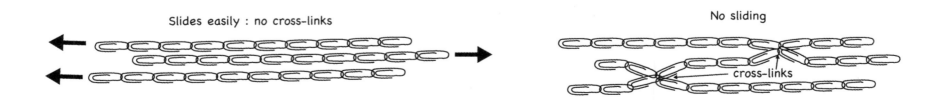

Experiment 10

Make it rise!

Materials needed:

    1 package (0.25 oz) active dry yeast
    sugar
    vegetable oil
    flour (4 cups)
    measuring cups
    measuring spoons
    marking pen
    two bowls

In this experiment the students will explore the activity of enzymes in active dry yeast. They will observe how yeast requires warm temperatures to make bread dough rise.

I. Think about it.

Help the students answer the questions in Section I. Their answers will vary. Sample answers are given.

1. List as many different types of molecules as you can.

acids, bases, salt, sugar, oils, water, enzymes

2. What kinds of molecules make food salty?

salt molecules

3. What kinds of molecules make cabbage juice turn red?

acid molecules

4. What kinds of molecules make cabbage juice turn green?

base molecules

5. What kinds of molecules are glue and starch made of?

long chains

6. What kinds of molecules do you think make bread rise?

salt molecules? sugar molecules? acid molecules?

II. Test it.

Help the students make two rounds of bread dough. One dough will be made using cold water and placed in the refrigerator to rise ["Dough B"]. The other dough will be made with warm water and placed in a warm place to rise ["Dough A"]. They should observe that "Dough A" rises and "Dough B" does not rise. Make sure that as you add warm water to "Dough A," the water is not too hot. Hot water will kill the yeast.

III. What did you discover?

Help the students answer the questions in Section III. They should observe a significant difference between "Dough A" and "Dough B." Help the students find words to describe what happened to the two doughs and how they were different. Help them connect the fact that one dough was made with cold water and kept in a cold place and the other dough was made with warm water and kept in a warm place. Point out to the students that temperature was the _only_ difference between the two doughs. Help them see that this one change was what caused one dough to rise and the other dough not to rise.

IV. Why?

Read and discuss Section IV with the students. Help them understand that yeast is a living thing and has very large molecules in it, called enzymes, that produce the gases needed for yeast to rise. Yeast contains enzymes that convert sugar to carbon dioxide and alcohol. This is called fermentation. The carbon dioxide that is produced during the fermentation process is what makes the bread rise. The alcohol is burned off during the baking process.

Explain to the students that there are many different kinds enzymes that do a variety of tasks. All of these are large, complicated molecules that are shaped in a particular way and designed to perform a particular function. There are enzymes that cut, enzymes that copy, enzymes that glue molecules together, and enzymes that read other molecules. Explain to the students that there are enzymes in their bodies that can only function within a narrow temperature range. The enzymes cannot function properly if their body temperature is either too hot or too cold.